Dedication

In solemn remembrance and heartfelt tribute, this book is dedicated to the over 10,000 Palestinian Children massacred by merciless onslaught of the Israeli military of the Palestinian people in the Genocide of Gaza during just the first 100 days. Their innocent lives, marked by unwarranted suffering and unimaginable loss, serve as a poignant reminder of the profound human cost of conflict.

May the collective cry's of these young innocent Children echo through the pages of this book, resonating across the globe, and inspiring a universal call for a stop to all wars, violence and all people's of earth to live in peace. In dedicating these words to the precious lives murdered, we aspire to ignite a transformative conversation about the imperative need to abandon violence as a means of resolving our differences.

May the memories of the Palestinian children be a catalyst for change, motivating people worldwide to seek paths to dialogue, diplomacy, and comprehensive peace with each other. In their honor, let us unite in our commitment to building a world where conflicts are resolved through courts of law, cooperation, and a shared

PEOPLEIZE

Chapter 4

Decolonizing Agriculture
People Before Profit

My Time, My Labor,
Our Earth, Our Money
WOBUNTU: I Am, Because We Are

By Einar Ourlove

PEOPLEIZE

This is a work of fiction. All of the characters, organizations, and events portrayed in this novel are either products of the author's imagination and are being used fictitiously in this novel.

Copyright ©

All rights reserved.

Our books may be purchased in bulk for promotional, educational, or business use. Please contact your local bookseller or us directly at info@einarourlove.com

www.einarourlove.com
www.peopleize.world

Originally published 2024

vision of peaceful coexistence. May their legacy be a guiding light, urging us all to work tirelessly towards a future where every child can grow and thrive in a world free from the shadows of violence and war.

Contents

Chapter i

Decolonizing Agriculture

The five fundamental needs crucial for human survival encompass:

1. **Water:** A vital element for sustaining life, water serves as a fundamental necessity for hydration, supporting bodily functions, and promoting overall health. Adequate access to clean and safe drinking water is imperative to ensure individuals remain adequately hydrated and healthy.

2. **Food:** Nutritious food provides the energy and essential nutrients necessary for the body to function properly. A balanced diet supports physical and mental health, ensuring individuals have the sustenance required for optimal bodily functions. Agriculture plays a pivotal role in providing a reliable food supply, cultivating crops and raising livestock to meet the nutritional needs of populations worldwide.

3. **Shelter:** Beyond mere protection from the elements, shelter offers a sanctuary where individuals can seek refuge from external threats and find respite. Providing a secure and stable environment, shelter is fundamental for promoting rest, relaxation, and a sense of security, contributing to overall

well-being. Agriculture contributes to the provision of shelter materials such as timber and other construction resources, further highlighting its crucial role in meeting human needs.

4. **Clothing:** Serving as more than mere attire, clothing plays a crucial role in safeguarding individuals against environmental factors and regulating body temperature. Appropriate clothing provides insulation and protection from the elements, ensuring comfort and well-being, particularly in diverse climates and conditions. Agriculture also provides fibers such as cotton and wool, which are essential for manufacturing clothing and textiles.

5. **Healthcare:** Access to comprehensive healthcare services is paramount for maintaining and promoting overall health. From preventive care measures to medical treatment and sanitation practices, healthcare services enable individuals to address health concerns, mitigate risks, and receive necessary medical attention in times of illness or injury. Agriculture contributes to healthcare indirectly by providing essential nutrients through food production, which is vital for supporting immune function and overall well-being.

It's important to note that despite the critical role agriculture plays in meeting the basic needs of local populations, disproportionate spending on military budgets often overshadows investments in agricultural development, highlighting a significant disparity in resource allocation.

Lets compare the grand theater of life, to a 400-meter track and field race. This metaphorical journey around the track becomes a powerful lens through which we scrutinize the inherent disparities in starting positions. Much like a race where individuals are positioned based on your inheritance at various starting points around the track, our lives unfold with some standing directly on the starting line, while others find themselves at a advantage starting 50 meters ahead and some even starting just a single step away from the finish line. Once the official signal the start of the race the individual standing just one step away from the finish line take a step forward and just like that they win the race and get the winning price. While the other participants are still running around the track, never having a chance to win the race no mater how fast they run.

The metaphor of the 400-meter race encapsulates the injustice of the circumstances into which individuals are born. This visual representation vividly illustrates the impact of factors such as family inheritance, birthplace, and socio-economic status on the starting positions in life's race. The central tenet of PEOPLEIZE is clear: No human being should claim ownership of the Earth or wield the power to dictate another's starting point in the unfolding journey of life on our Earth as a people.

If each person's starting point is based on when, where, and to whom you are born, then this injustice is perpetuated by the current monetary system created by colonial countries that have created countries with disregard for the local indigenous population. Of the current 194 countries in the world, 121 were created without any regard for the local indigenous population and are still controlled by the same colonial countries' manipulation of the monetary system they have installed, ensuring that future generations are always at a disadvantage from birth without any possibility to recover from this oppression.

Here is a list of countries that were created by European exploration, colonization, settlement, and without any regard for the local indigenous original population: United States, Canada, Mexico, Brazil, Argentina, Chile, Peru, Colombia, Venezuela, Bolivia, Uruguay, Paraguay, Ecuador, Australia, New Zealand, South Africa, Egypt, Algeria, Angola, Mozambique, Democratic Republic of the Congo, Republic of the Congo, Nigeria, Ghana, Kenya, Tanzania, South Sudan, Sudan, Ethiopia, Somalia, Morocco, Tunisia, Libya, Namibia, Botswana, Zimbabwe, Zambia, Malawi, Uganda, Rwanda, Burundi, Cameroon, Ivory Coast, Senegal, Guinea, Sierra Leone, Liberia, Gambia, Guinea-Bissau, Cape Verde, Mauritania, Western Sahara, Chad, Niger, Mali,

Burkina Faso, Togo, Benin, Central African Republic, Gabon, Equatorial Guinea, Seychelles, Mauritius, Comoros, Madagascar, Maldives, Sri Lanka, Bangladesh, Myanmar, Malaysia, Indonesia, Philippines, Brunei, East Timor, India, Pakistan, Afghanistan, Nepal, Bhutan, Papua New Guinea, Solomon Islands, Fiji, Vanuatu, Samoa, Tonga, Tuvalu, Kiribati, Marshall Islands, Palau, Micronesia, Nauru, Cook Islands, Niue, Grenada, Saint Kitts and Nevis, Saint Lucia, Saint Vincent and the Grenadines, Antigua and Barbuda, Dominica, Bahamas, Barbados, Jamaica, Trinidad and Tobago, Guyana, Suriname, Belize, Haiti, Dominican Republic, Cuba, Costa Rica, Panama, El Salvador, Honduras, Nicaragua, Guatemala, Paraguay, and Uruguay,

These new countries, created from land colonization, left the indigenous population to be just slaves until independence, and then controlled using colonial treaties to exploit the raw materials for European benefits, economic inequality practices, and constant disregard for the rights of the local indigenous population, which still remain to this day. By removing this injustice that was created when colonial countries created borders without any regard for the local indigenous culture and population, only to benefit their own selfish European greed, the challenge now is decolonizing these colonization practices and empowering the indigenous population to focus on their community growth and not just the development of Europe. In this book, let's look at 4 countries: South Africa, Tanzania, Germany, and Thailand, and their current agricultural landscape and how an implementation of the people-sized concept would be more holistic and sustainable for the indigenous population and the Earth.

Here is a table overview with data of the four countries:

Aspect	South Africa	Tanzania	Germany	Thailand
Main Crops	Maize, sugarcane, citrus fruits, grapes, wheat.	Maize, cassava, rice, coffee, cashew nuts.	Wheat, barley, sugar beets, potatoes, hops.	Rice, cassava, rubber, sugarcane, palm oil.
Main Livestock	Cattle, sheep, goats, poultry.	Cattle, sheep, goats, poultry.	Cattle, pigs, poultry, dairy cows.	Pigs, poultry, cattle, fish, shrimp.
Ownership	Majority of farms are locally owned, with some international investment in large-scale commercial operations.	Majority of farms are smallholder-owned, with limited international investment.	Farm ownership is diverse, including family-owned farms, cooperatives, and corporate entities.	Majority of farms are smallholder-owned, with increasing industrial-scale farming operations.
Income	Smallholder farmers may struggle with low incomes and access to resources. Commercial farmers may have higher earnings but face challenges like market fluctuations.	Smallholder farmers often operate on a subsistence basis, with modest earnings and challenges accessing inputs and markets. Large-scale farmers may have higher profits but still face risks such as weather and policy changes.	Farming is generally profitable, with modern technology and government support. However, smaller farms may face challenges due to high costs and competition.	Agriculture provides income for millions, with varying levels of profitability across different sectors.

Government Support	Various government programs aim to support smallholder farmers but effectiveness may vary. Estimated government support: $500 million. Examples: Land Redistribution for Agricultural Development (LRAD), Comprehensive Agricultural Support Programme (CASP).	Government initiatives focus on improving access to inputs, extension services, and market information for smallholder farmers. Estimated government support: $200 million. Examples: Agricultural Sector Development Program (ASDP), National Irrigation Development Plan (NIDP).	Government provides significant support through subsidies, incentives, and technical assistance programs. Estimated government support: $10 billion. Examples: Common Agricultural Policy (CAP), Rural Development Program (RDP).	Government provides support through various schemes and policies, including price support programs and subsidies.
Land Ownership	Land ownership patterns are complex, with historical disparities and ongoing debates about land reform.	Land tenure systems vary, with smallholder farmers often relying on customary or informal arrangements.	Land ownership is regulated, with a mix of private ownership, tenancy, and leasing arrangements.	Land ownership is relatively concentrated, with significant government intervention in land distribution and management.
Technology Adoption	Technology adoption varies, with larger farms often utilizing modern equipment and practices.	Limited access to technology and mechanization, especially among smallholder farmers.	High level of technology adoption, including precision farming, automation, and digital tools.	Adoption of modern agricultural practices is increasing, particularly in commercial farming sectors.
Market Access	Market access can be challenging for smallholder farmers due to limited infrastructure and market information.	Market access is limited, with smallholder farmers often relying on informal markets and middlemen.	Farmers generally have good market access through established supply chains and marketing channels.	Well-developed agricultural infrastructure facilitates market access for farmers.

Environment al Concerns	Environmental sustainability is a growing focus, with efforts to promote conservation agriculture and sustainable practices.	Environmental sustainability is a concern, with challenges related to deforestation, soil degradation, and water management.	Environmental sustainability is prioritized, with strict regulations and incentives for sustainable farming practices.	Environmental sustainability is a concern, particularly regarding water management, pesticide use, and deforestation.
Labor Practices	Labor practices vary, with smallholder farmers often relying on family labor and occasional hired help.	Labor practices vary, with smallholder farmers often relying on family labor and occasional hired help.	Labor practices are regulated, with a focus on fair wages, worker rights, and safety standards.	Labor practices vary, with a significant portion of the workforce engaged in agricultural activities.
Estimated People Earning Income	Approximately 3.8 million people employed in agriculture and related activities.	Agriculture employs the majority of the population, with millions of smallholder farmers and rural households relying on farming for income.	Agriculture provides employment for a significant portion of the population, with estimates suggesting hundreds of thousands of people working in the agricultural sector.	Agriculture employs millions of people, contributing significantly to rural livelihoods.
Estimated Number of Registered Farms	Around 35,000 registered commercial farms.	Estimated to be in the millions, including both registered and unregistered farms.	Approximately 285,000 registered farms.	Data not available.
Agriculture Needs Met (%)	Livestock: 80%, Vegetables: 70%, Fruits: 60%, Dairy: 75%, Eggs: 70%, Potatoes: 80%, Sugar: 60%, Honey: 50%, Corn: 70%, Wheat: 80%	Livestock: 70%, Vegetables: 50%, Fruits: 40%, Dairy: 60%, Eggs: 50%, Potatoes: 60%, Sugar: 40%, Honey: 30%, Corn: 60%, Wheat: 70%	Livestock: 90%, Vegetables: 80%, Fruits: 70%, Dairy: 95%, Eggs: 90%, Potatoes: 90%, Sugar: 80%, Honey: 70%, Corn: 95%, Wheat: 90%	Data not available.
Estimated Population	Approximately 60 million.	Approximately 60 million.	Approximately 83 million.	Approximately 70 million.
Military Personnel	Approximately 78,000 active personnel.	Approximately 27,000 active personnel.	Approximately 180,000 active personnel.	Approximately 306,000 active personnel.
Military Budget (USD)	Approximately $4.5 billion.	Approximately $900 million.	Approximately $60 billion.	Approximately $7.3 billion.

In the face of global challenges, how can each country ensure its prosperity while prioritizing the well-being, growth, and sustainability of its citizens through collaborative efforts on a global scale?

My Time and My Labor:

Embracing the principle of equality, we propose a transformative approach to labor compensation. Upon reaching adulthood, every individual will receive an equal salary, irrespective of their occupation or position. This groundbreaking initiative not only fosters global equality but also liberates individuals from the shackles of survival-based work, empowering them to pursue careers aligned with their passions and aspirations. By placing people before profit, we forge a path towards a more equitable and fulfilling society.

Our Earth and Our Money:

Recognizing the intrinsic value of our planet's resources, we advocate for the collective stewardship of land as a communal asset. No longer will land be held captive by corporate or individual interests; instead, it will be utilized for the collective benefit of communities and global collaborations, ensuring the sustainable utilization of natural resources for generations to come.

WOBUNTU:

Grounded in the African philosophy of interconnectedness, WOBUNTU underscores the importance of prioritizing people over profit. By fostering collaboration and solidarity, we can collectively strive towards a sustainable world free from exploitation and inequality. Embracing the ethos of **"I Am, Because We Are,"** we recognize that our collective well-being is intrinsically linked to the well-being of others, inspiring us to work towards a common vision of prosperity and harmony.

Understanding the fallacy of our current monetary system, which perpetuates inequality and exploitation, we advocate for the transition to a PEOPLEIZE monetary system. By acknowledging that the value of paper money is merely a human construct, we can harness its potential to create a positive impact on society. Drawing inspiration from the provision of resources to soldiers, who receive salaries, education, equipment, and training for their work, we advocate for extending similar support to all individuals. We affirm that every individual deserves access to the essential resources necessary for survival, including education, healthcare, and livelihood opportunities.

This paradigm shift towards a PEOPLEIZE monetary system prioritizes the support and empowerment of individuals rather than exerting control over them. By leveraging our existing financial infrastructure, we can redirect resources towards initiatives that promote sustainability and prioritize the well-being of people over profit. In particular, we emphasize the critical role of agriculture and farmers in sustaining communities worldwide. Rather than bolstering profit-driven corporations, we champion initiatives that prioritize sustainability and equitable access to resources, ensuring that the basic needs of all individuals are met while fostering a more resilient and equitable society.

The essence of the PEOPLEIZE concept lies in its commitment to equity and empowerment, envisioning a society where every individual is valued equally and has the opportunity to pursue their passions and dreams without the constraints of financial disparity. At its core, PEOPLEIZE advocates for paying every person the same amount for their work, ensuring that individuals are not merely working to survive but are enabled to thrive and contribute meaningfully to their communities.

By implementing a global standard salary of 50,000, and establishing currency equality worldwide, PEOPLEIZE liberates individuals from the burden of financial insecurity, allowing them to choose their career paths based on personal fulfillment rather than monetary gain. This transformative approach fosters a culture of innovation and creativity, as individuals are encouraged to pursue their interests and talents, knowing that their livelihood is assured.

Moreover, PEOPLEIZE recognizes the interconnectedness of communities on a local, national, and global scale, advocating for collaborative efforts that transcend geographical boundaries. By nurturing local community collaborations, which in turn align with national and global initiatives, PEOPLEIZE promotes solidarity and mutual support, harnessing the collective potential of diverse communities to address shared challenges and advance common goals.

With each person receiving equal compensation, the government assumes a pivotal role in facilitating societal frameworks that promote collective well-being and prosperity. By reallocating resources previously dedicated to perpetuating economic disparity, governments can invest in essential services such as education and healthcare, laying the foundation for a more equitable and inclusive society.

Under the PEOPLEIZE model, the cost barriers to education are dismantled, enabling the construction of schools with smaller class sizes to facilitate personalized learning experiences. Similarly, the healthcare system undergoes significant improvements, with increased access to hospitals and medical facilities in both urban and rural areas. By removing the financial barriers associated with land ownership and loans, PEOPLEIZE fosters a more equitable distribution of resources, ensuring that every individual has access to opportunities for personal and professional growth.

Ultimately, the PEOPLEIZE concept transcends mere economic principles, advocating for a fundamental shift in societal values towards equality, justice, and collective well-being. By valuing each person's contributions equally and fostering an environment of mutual respect and support, PEOPLEIZE paves the way for a more harmonious and sustainable future for all.

When it comes to consumer choices, whether you opt for an SUV or a standard car, the decision is entirely yours, as both options are priced and valued equally. This egalitarian approach eliminates the societal fixation on 'bigger is better,' fostering a culture where car companies prioritize sustainability over profit margins. By shifting the focus away from size and extravagance, manufacturers are encouraged to invest in eco-friendly technologies and practices, ensuring that every vehicle produced contributes to a greener, more sustainable future.

Turning our attention to agriculture, it's essential to recognize that land is a communal asset, belonging to the collective community rather than any individual or corporation. While companies may utilize this land to cultivate crops and provide food for the community, it's imperative that they do so with a commitment to local sustainability and equitable distribution. It's nonsensical for a company to lay claim to farmers worldwide, producing goods exclusively for distant European markets while neglecting the needs of the local community.

Furthermore, the establishment of monopolies within the agricultural sector stifles innovation and undermines efforts towards sustainability. Instead of monopolizing resources, companies should prioritize collaboration with local farms in diverse regions, pooling knowledge and resources to cultivate a more sustainable Earth. By embracing cooperation over competition, we can work towards a future where agriculture serves the needs of communities worldwide, fostering resilience and ecological harmony.

Moreover, it's crucial to reevaluate the value systems underpinning investment and financial markets. The worth of investors' assets is often determined by virtual paper money, detached from tangible value and real-world sustainability. By redefining the value of currency to prioritize environmental and social well-being, we can redirect financial resources towards initiatives that promote a sustainable future for all. After all, the true measure of wealth lies not in monetary assets but in the health and vitality of our planet and its inhabitants.

This does not imply advocating for a society where individuals work without compensation;

rather, it entails the establishment of a socio-economic system that upholds equality and dismantles the pervasive colonial mindset that has long plagued our communities. Historically, we've been conditioned to chase after a proverbial carrot dangled in front of us, perpetuating a cycle wherein the vast majority of the population remains trapped in perpetual poverty, while a privileged few reap the benefits of their labor.

For centuries, our societies have been structured around a hierarchical framework, rooted in colonialist ideologies and upheld by systems of power and control. This hierarchical structure has been perpetuated not only through economic exploitation but also through deeply ingrained religious beliefs that justify and reinforce existing inequalities.

It's time to confront this reality and acknowledge that our current socio-economic system is fundamentally flawed and unjust. After 2000 years of societal evolution, it's imperative that we recognize the inherent inequities ingrained within our systems and strive towards building a society founded on principles of genuine equality and justice.

By challenging the colonial mindset and dismantling systems of oppression, we can pave the way for a more inclusive and equitable society. This requires reimagining our economic structures, prioritizing the needs of all members of society over the interests of a privileged few, and creating avenues for meaningful participation and empowerment for marginalized communities.

In doing so, we can forge a path towards a future where every individual is afforded equal opportunities and access to resources, regardless of their background or circumstances. It's time to break free from the chains of colonialism and forge a new path towards a truly equitable and just society for all.

We, the people, have the time and labor to say no more; we want equality and to stop running after a carrot that we will not reach.

The process for agriculture will revolutionize the traditional farming model by establishing hyper-local farms, which are collaborative efforts among a small group of dedicated farmers. These farms will serve as the backbone of local food production, aiming to sustainably feed an estimated 10,000 people within their immediate vicinity, thereby reducing reliance on distant food sources and minimizing carbon footprint.

Operating under the innovative PEOPLEIZE model, these hyper-local farms will be privately owned, yet fundamentally community-oriented. By ensuring that all participating farmers and owners receive equitable compensation, including salaries, healthcare benefits, educational opportunities, specialized training, and access to modern equipment, the focus shifts from mere survival to fostering a culture of excellence in sustainable agricultural practices.

Moreover, these farms will prioritize environmental stewardship and resource conservation, implementing techniques such as crop rotation, organic farming methods, and water-saving irrigation systems. Through ongoing education and training programs, farmers will continually enhance their skills and adapt to evolving best practices in the field.

Integral to the success of this model is the establishment of strong partnerships with local supermarkets and food processors. Rather than relying on distant supply chains, supermarkets will be incentivized to procure locally grown produce and goods. This shift not only ensures fresher, more nutritious food for consumers but also bolsters the local economy by supporting small-scale producers.

Furthermore, by processing food locally instead of shipping it for external processing, the hyper-local model minimizes transportation costs and reduces carbon emissions associated with long-distance transport. This streamlined approach to food production and distribution fosters resilience within the local food system, insulating it from external market fluctuations and disruptions.

In essence, the hyper-local model for agriculture and food production represents a paradigm shift towards community empowerment, sustainability, and economic equity. By keeping production and consumption within local boundaries, it fosters job creation, promotes environmental sustainability, and mitigates the inequalities perpetuated by globalized food systems. Through collective action and innovation, communities can reclaim control over their food sources and build a more resilient, equitable future for all.

In the forthcoming chapters, we will delve into a comprehensive exploration of strategies aimed at realizing sustainable agriculture. Our focus extends beyond the confines of local communities to embrace global collaboration founded on principles of equality and environmental stewardship. By elucidating practical approaches and innovative solutions, we aim to pave the way towards a sustainable future that benefits all individuals, irrespective of geographical boundaries or socioeconomic status. Through collective action and a commitment to fostering harmony between humanity and the planet, we aspire to cultivate a world where agriculture thrives in tandem with ecological preservation and social equity.

Chapter ii

PEOPLEIZE Livestock & Crop Integrating Farming

In the intricate tapestry of farming, the practice of "mixed farming" or "integrated farming" represents a harmonious blend of different livestock species, each contributing unique behaviors, dietary preferences, and habitat interactions to create a mutually beneficial ecosystem. Here are some vivid examples showcasing the synergistic relationships among various livestock combinations:

1. **Cattle and Sheep**: In a bucolic pasture setting, cattle and sheep coexist in perfect harmony. While cattle graze on grasses with gusto, sheep exhibit a more discerning palate, selecting choice vegetation. Together, they efficiently utilize the pasture, preventing overgrazing and nurturing a diverse ecosystem.

2. **Chickens and Pigs**: Amidst the rustling fields, chickens and pigs engage in a delightful dance of symbiosis. Following pigs in rotational grazing systems, chickens eagerly scratch and peck through the pig manure, feasting on insects and larvae. This not only aids in manure decomposition, reducing odors

and flies, but also provides chickens with a nutritious supplementary food source.

3. **Goats and Cattle**: Across sprawling pastures, goats and cattle forge an alliance against unruly brush and weeds. With goats exhibiting a penchant for shrubs and woody vegetation, they expertly navigate the terrain, controlling undesirable plant growth that cattle might overlook. This partnership ensures a balanced forage utilization across the pasture landscape.

4. **Ducks and Fish**: In tranquil aquaculture ponds, ducks and fish partake in a delicate ecological ballet. Ducks, with their voracious appetite for insects and algae, glide across the water's surface, diligently controlling pests and fertilizing the water with their droppings. This synergistic relationship fosters improved water quality and heightened productivity for the resident fish population.

5. **Rabbits and Chickens**: Above bustling chicken coops, rabbits reside in elevated hutches, contributing to a cycle of nutrient recycling. Rabbit waste gracefully falls through the hutches, enriching the soil below with nitrogen-rich fertilizer for the chickens. Meanwhile, both species share grazing areas, with rabbits nibbling on lower vegetation while chickens diligently hunt for insects.

6. **Horses and Cattle**: Amidst swaying grasslands, horses and cattle graze side by side, each playing a vital role in maintaining pasture diversity. While cattle favor longer grasses, horses, with their discerning palates, selectively graze on different grass and forb species. Together, they weave a tapestry of biodiversity across the pasture landscape.

7. **Bees and Livestock**: Amidst the vibrant blooms of mixed farms, honeybees flit from flower to flower, pollinating crops and forage plants. Although not traditional livestock, bees play a crucial role in enhancing agricultural productivity through their invaluable pollination services. Moreover, they thrive amidst the diverse floral resources found on mixed farms, contributing to the richness and abundance of the ecosystem.

These examples illustrate the intricate interplay among different livestock species in fostering a balanced and sustainable farming ecosystem, where each participant contributes to the overall health and productivity of the farm.

There are diverse examples of crop combinations that illustrate the synergistic benefits of integrating different plant species within the agricultural landscape, either grown together or in rotation with livestock:

1. **Legumes and Grasses**: Combining leguminous crops like clover, alfalfa, or

soybeans with grasses such as ryegrass or fescue is a classic pairing in pasture systems. Legumes fix atmospheric nitrogen, enriching the soil fertility, while grasses provide structural support, prevent soil erosion, and create a balanced ecosystem conducive to grazing livestock.

2. **Corn and Soybeans**: The rotation of corn and soybeans is a prevalent practice in modern agriculture. Soybeans contribute nitrogen to the soil, benefiting subsequent corn crops, while corn residues enrich the soil with organic matter and act as a natural weed suppressor during the soybean growing season.

3. **Root Vegetables and Leafy Greens**: Intercropping root crops like carrots, beets, or radishes with leafy greens such as lettuce, spinach, or kale offers multiple benefits. Root vegetables break up compacted soil, improving soil structure, while leafy greens provide ground cover, reducing weed competition, and conserving soil moisture.

4. **Grains and Forage Crops**: Growing grains like oats, barley, or wheat alongside forage crops such as clover or alfalfa is advantageous for both livestock and soil health. Grains offer additional income or feed for livestock, while forage crops enhance soil fertility, provide grazing options, and contribute to hay production.

5. **Fruit Trees and Cover Crops**: Intercropping fruit trees like apples, peaches, or cherries with cover crops such as legumes, grasses, or clover presents a symbiotic relationship. Cover crops suppress weeds, reduce erosion, and improve soil health, while fruit trees offer a profitable long-term cash crop.

6. **Herbs and Flowers**: Interplanting culinary herbs and flowers with vegetables or fruits serves multiple ecological functions. Herbs and flowers attract pollinators, repel pests, and enhance biodiversity, thus promoting a healthier ecosystem and improving overall crop yield and quality.

7. **Perennial and Annual Crops**: Integrating perennial crops like asparagus, rhubarb, or berries with annual crops like tomatoes, peppers, or cucumbers creates a dynamic agricultural system. Perennial crops provide long-term stability, habitat for beneficial insects, and continuous harvests, while annual crops offer diversity in produce and short-term yields.

These examples underscore the versatility and adaptability of integrated farming practices to various environmental conditions, market demands, and farm management approaches. Intercropping and crop rotation strategies maximize yield, minimize pest and disease pressure, and enhance overall farm sustainability by fostering a resilient and diversified agricultural ecosystem.

Integrating livestock farming with crop farming represents a holistic approach that harmonizes the symbiotic relationship between plants and animals, mirroring the intricate balance found in natural ecosystems. This integrated method, often referred to as agroecology or agroecosystem design, encompasses various strategies aimed at optimizing agricultural productivity while fostering environmental sustainability. Here's an in-depth exploration of the ways in which livestock farming can be seamlessly integrated into crop farming to achieve mutual benefits:

1. **Grazing Cover Crops**: By allowing livestock to graze on cover crops planted between cash crop seasons, farmers can harness the dual benefits of soil improvement and forage production. Cover crops like clover, vetch, or rye not only enhance soil health by reducing erosion and suppressing weeds but also provide nutritious forage for grazing animals. Moreover, grazing livestock help terminate cover crops naturally, eliminating the need for herbicides or mechanical tillage.

2. **Manure Fertilization**: The nutrient-rich manure produced by livestock serves as a valuable natural fertilizer for crops. By integrating livestock into crop rotations, farmers can recycle nutrients effectively,

spreading animal waste onto fields to replenish soil fertility. This sustainable practice reduces reliance on synthetic fertilizers, enhances soil health and structure, and promotes nutrient cycling within the agroecosystem.

3. **Intensive Rotational Grazing**: Employing intensive rotational grazing systems on pastureland adjacent to crop fields optimizes pasture utilization while benefiting soil health. Rotational grazing not only improves forage quality and reduces weed pressure but also enriches the soil with nutrient-rich manure deposited by grazing livestock. This nutrient cycling enhances soil fertility, fostering healthier crop growth and productivity in subsequent rotations.

4. **Agroforestry**: Integrating trees or shrubs with crops and livestock in agroforestry systems offers multiple benefits ranging from shade provision to enhanced nutrient cycling. In silvopasture systems, trees or shrubs provide shelter and additional forage options for grazing livestock while contributing to soil fertility. Livestock graze on grasses and legumes beneath the tree canopy, promoting nutrient cycling and enhancing soil health.

5. **Livestock Integration in No-Till Systems**: Incorporating livestock into no-till or reduced tillage systems promotes soil health and erosion control. Livestock trampling and

manure deposition help incorporate crop residues into the soil, increasing organic matter content and improving soil structure. This enhances water infiltration and nutrient cycling, ultimately leading to improved soil health and productivity.

6. **Biogas Production**: Utilizing livestock waste and crop residues for biogas production through anaerobic digestion offers a renewable energy source for heating, electricity generation, or cooking. Biogas production reduces reliance on fossil fuels, mitigates greenhouse gas emissions, and promotes energy self-sufficiency on farms.

7. **Integrated Pest Management (IPM)**: Livestock play a crucial role in pest control within crop fields through integrated pest management strategies. For instance, chickens can be introduced to orchards to forage for insects and pests, reducing the need for chemical pesticides. This natural pest control method minimizes environmental impact while maintaining crop health and productivity.

These integrated approaches not only bolster farm productivity and sustainability but also serve as catalysts for promoting ecological harmony within communities. By fostering biodiversity, improving soil health, and maximizing resource efficiency within the agroecosystem, these practices contribute to the overall well-being of the environment and the communities that depend on it.

In the upcoming chapter, we will delve into four illustrative examples that highlight the manifold advantages of these integrated farming methods. From enhancing crop yields to minimizing environmental impact, these approaches not only prove to be more cost-effective but also play a pivotal role in promoting equality among people and communities. Through equitable access to resources and opportunities, these practices empower individuals to actively participate in sustainable agriculture, thereby fostering a more inclusive and resilient community fabric.

Chapter iii

The PEOPLEIZE Agriculture Collaboration

In our pursuit of sustainable agricultural practices, it is imperative to design integrated farming systems that cater to the diverse needs of local communities while prioritizing environmental conservation and community resilience. Each region presents unique challenges and opportunities, calling for tailored approaches to maximize productivity and sustainability. Here, we embark on a journey to envision integrated farms tailored to the needs of small communities in Germany, Thailand, South Africa, and Tanzania.

Integrated Farming in Germany: Germany's integrated farm is conceived as a harmonious blend of livestock and crop production methods, meticulously designed to cater to the needs of a small community comprising approximately 10,000 individuals. Envisioned within the verdant landscapes of Germany, this farm is poised to produce an array of dairy products, meats, fish, eggs, cereals, vegetables, fruits, and other essential crops sustainably. Our vision extends beyond mere production; we aim to foster a symbiotic relationship between agriculture and the environment, leveraging sustainable practices to nurture both land and livelihoods.

Integrated Farming in Thailand: Nestled amidst the lush greenery of Thailand, our integrated farm stands as a testament to the country's rich agricultural heritage and biodiversity. Here, we envisage a holistic farming approach that integrates dairy, meat, egg, fish, and crop production to meet the needs of a local community of 10,000 people. Drawing inspiration from traditional farming practices and indigenous knowledge, our farm endeavors to uphold the principles of sustainability and self-sufficiency while embracing the challenges of tropical agriculture.

Integrated Farming in South Africa: In the vibrant landscapes of South Africa, our integrated farm emerges as a beacon of agricultural innovation and community resilience. With a focus on dairy, meat, egg, fish, and crop production, our farm seeks to address the diverse dietary needs of a small community while championing environmental stewardship and social equity. Rooted in the rich tapestry of South African agriculture, our vision encompasses a harmonious coexistence between nature and nurture, where sustainable practices pave the way for a prosperous future.

Integrated Farming in Tanzania: Embraced by the sweeping plains of Tanzania, our integrated farm embodies the spirit of resilience and resourcefulness inherent to the region. Here, amidst the vibrant tapestry of diverse cultures and landscapes, we envision a farm that integrates dairy, meat, egg, fish, and crop production to sustainably support a local community of 10,000 individuals. Guided by principles of conservation and community empowerment, our farm endeavors to forge a path towards food security and environmental sustainability in Tanzania.

As we embark on this journey, we recognize the intrinsic connection between agriculture, ecology, and human well-being. Through collaborative efforts and a commitment to sustainable practices, we aim to cultivate a future where agriculture thrives in harmony with nature, nourishing both body and soul. Join us as we explore the possibilities of integrated farming and chart a course towards a more resilient and sustainable future for all.

The framework underpinning these farms is built upon principles of equity, sustainability, and community empowerment. Central to this framework is the notion that every farmer receives equal compensation, access to training, education, equipment, and land resources. By leveling the playing field in this manner, we aim to foster a culture of collaboration and mutual support among farmers, ensuring that each individual has the tools and resources needed to thrive.

A key aspect of this integrated approach is the multifaceted utilization of land, where various agricultural activities are harmoniously interwoven to maximize productivity while minimizing environmental impact. By integrating multiple uses for the land, such as crop cultivation, livestock grazing, agroforestry, and conservation practices, we seek to create resilient and biodiverse ecosystems that support both agricultural production and ecosystem services.

Moreover, the processing of agricultural produce is strategically localized within or near the community or region of farms. By establishing processing facilities in close proximity to the farms, we eliminate the need for long-distance transportation of perishable goods, thereby reducing carbon emissions, minimizing food waste, and lowering overall costs. This localized approach not only enhances the economic viability of small-scale farmers but also strengthens the resilience of local food systems.

Furthermore, the development of electricity infrastructure is tailored to meet the specific needs of community farms, emphasizing a hyper-local and small-scale approach. By ensuring reliable access to electricity, we empower farmers and workers with essential services and amenities, such as irrigation systems, refrigeration units, and processing equipment. This integrated approach to infrastructure development not only enhances agricultural productivity but also fosters socio-economic development and prosperity within the community. The infrastructure is designed to be self-sufficient and stand-alone, ensuring sustainability and resilience in the face of external disruptions. By prioritizing localized solutions, we create a robust foundation for agricultural operations that is responsive to the unique needs and challenges of each community farm.

Additionally, farms and workers create unions to ensure cooperation and collaboration between members within the local community organization. These unions serve as platforms for collective decision-making, resource sharing, and skill development, fostering a sense of solidarity and mutual support among farmers and workers.

Each union will send two representative to the central government annually, ensuring collaboration with the larger community in the country. These representatives will advocate for the needs and interests of their respective industries and communities, contributing to the formulation of national policies and initiatives that promote sustainability across all sectors. Moreover, these representatives are selected randomly each year from the union members, ensuring a fair and inclusive representation of diverse voices at the national level.

In essence, the framework for these community farms is grounded in the principles of inclusivity, sustainability, and self-reliance. By prioritizing equitable access to resources, localized processing, and tailored infrastructure development, we aim to cultivate thriving agricultural communities that serve as models of resilience and sustainability for generations to come. Through active participation in the democratic process and collective action at both local and national levels, these community farms contribute to the advancement of a more sustainable and equitable society.

Energy Production:

The PEOPLEIZE Agriculture Future envisions each community as a self-sufficient entity, harnessing renewable energy sources to power its farm operations. Solar panels will adorn the rooftops of farm buildings, soaking up the sun's rays to generate electricity for various needs, from lighting the farm facilities to running machinery and equipment. Additionally, wind turbines strategically positioned across the farm's expansive landscape will capture the power of the wind, further contributing to the energy production. This reliance on renewable energy not only reduces the farm's carbon footprint but also ensures a reliable and sustainable source of power, independent of fluctuating energy prices.

Waste Management and Recycling:

In line with the principles of sustainability and resource efficiency, the farm will implement comprehensive waste management and recycling practices. Organic waste generated from crop residues, food scraps, and animal manure will be meticulously composted to produce nutrient-rich fertilizer for use in crop production, closing the loop of nutrient cycling within the farm ecosystem. Additionally, biogas digesters will be employed to convert organic waste into biogas through anaerobic digestion, providing a renewable energy source for heating, cooking, and other on-farm energy needs. This innovative approach not only reduces waste sent to landfills but also generates valuable energy resources from otherwise discarded materials.

Water Treatment and Recycling:

Water conservation and management will be paramount in the PEOPLEIZE Agriculture Future, with each community implementing advanced water treatment and recycling systems. Greywater from farm facilities and residences will undergo treatment processes, such as filtration and purification, to ensure its quality for irrigation and other agricultural purposes. Rainwater harvesting systems will collect and store rainwater runoff from rooftops and paved surfaces, supplementing irrigation water needs during dry periods and reducing reliance on groundwater sources. Additionally, innovative techniques like aquaponics and hydroponics will be utilized to maximize water efficiency in crop production, further minimizing water wastage and promoting sustainable agricultural practices.

Rainwater Collection and Atmospheric Water Harvesting:

To augment its water resources, each farm will incorporate rainwater collection systems to capture precipitation for various agricultural purposes. Large cisterns and storage tanks will be strategically positioned to collect rainwater runoff from rooftops and other impervious surfaces, providing a supplemental water source for irrigation, livestock watering, and other on-farm needs. Moreover, innovative atmospheric water harvesting technologies will be deployed to extract moisture from the air, particularly in regions with high humidity levels. This approach harnesses atmospheric moisture through condensation, further enhancing the farm's water resilience and reducing dependency on external water sources.

By integrating renewable energy production, waste management, water treatment and recycling, rainwater collection, and atmospheric water harvesting into farm operations, each community within the PEOPLEIZE Agriculture Future will embody self-sufficiency and resilience. These holistic approaches not only reduce environmental impact but also enhance the farm's capacity to thrive independently while fostering a harmonious relationship with the surrounding ecosystem.

These farms can function as one farm or as individually owned farms, collaborating and sharing the same land.

Let's design an integrated farm that incorporates various livestock and crop production methods to meet the needs of a small community of 10,000 people in **Germany**. This farm will aim to produce dairy products, meats, fish, eggs, corn, corn, wheat, sugar, vegetable, fruits, and other crops sustainably.

Here's a rough outline of the farm setup:

Integrated Farm Setup for a Community in Germany:

1. Dairy Production:

a. The farm will have a dairy herd of approximately 50 dairy cows, such as Holsteins or Jerseys.
b. Cows will be grazed on pasture during the growing season and supplemented with stored forages during winter.
c. Manure from dairy cows will be composted and used as fertilizer for crop fields.

2. Meat Production:

a. The farm will raise approximately 200 pigs and 200 chickens for meat production.

b. Pigs will be raised in a rotational grazing system or on pasture areas not suitable for crop production.
c. Chickens will be raised in mobile coops following behind grazing livestock or integrated into orchards and vineyards.
d. Cows and other animals can also be incorporated for meat production based on local population needs

3. Fish Production:

a. The farm will incorporate small aquaculture operations, potentially producing fish such as trout in ponds or recirculating aquaculture systems.
b. Fish waste will be used to fertilize crop fields or incorporated into compost.

4. Egg Production:

a. The farm will maintain a flock of approximately 500 laying hens to produce eggs for the community.
b. Hens will be raised in mobile coops or pasture pens, following behind grazing livestock or integrated into orchards and vineyards.

5. Crop Production:

a. The farm will grow crops such as corn, wheat, sugar beets, vegetables (e.g., potatoes, carrots, cabbage), and fruits (e.g., apples, cherries, berries) to supplement the livestock diet and provide food for the community.

b. Sustainable practices such as crop rotation, cover cropping, and integrated pest management will be employed.

c. Greenhouses or high tunnels may be used for year-round vegetable production.

6. Honey Production:

a. The farm will maintain beehives for honey production, utilizing diverse floral resources from crop fields, hedgerows, and wildflowers.

b. Honey production will contribute to pollination services and provide an additional income source for the farm.

7. Sugar Production:

a. The farm will allocate a portion of land for sugar beet cultivation.

b. Sugar beets will be processed to produce sugar for both on-farm consumption and potential sale to the local community.

8. Agroforestry and Perennial Crops:

a. The farm will incorporate agroforestry systems with fruit and nut trees, such as apple, pear, walnut, and hazelnut trees, providing additional food sources and habitat for wildlife.

b. Perennial crops such as asparagus, rhubarb, and berries will be integrated into crop rotations.

Estimates for Farm Size in Acres:

a. Dairy Production: Approximately 50-100 acres.
b. Meat Production (Pigs and Chickens): Approximately 50-100 acres.
c. Fish Production: Approximately 5-10 acres.
d. Egg Production: Approximately 5 acres.
e. Crop Production (including vegetables and fruits): Approximately 200-300 acres.
f. Honey Production: Integrated within the existing farm area.
g. Sugar Production: Additional land allocation depending on scale.

Total: Adding up these estimates, the farm might require approximately 462-817 acres of land to support the various livestock and crop enterprises, including honey and sugar production.

This integrated farm setup aims to provide a diverse range of food products sustainably while promoting environmental stewardship and community resilience in Germany.

Integrated farm for a small community of 10,000 people in **Thailand**. Here's how it might look:

Integrated Farm Setup for a Community in Thailand:

1. Dairy Production:

a. The farm will have a dairy herd of approximately 50 dairy cows, including native breeds such as Thai Holstein or Thai Native Cattle.
b. Cows will be grazed on pasture during the growing season and supplemented with stored forages during the dry season.
c. Manure from dairy cows will be composted and used as fertilizer for crop fields.

2. Meat Production:

a. The farm will raise approximately 200 pigs and 200 chickens for meat production.
b. Pigs will be raised in a rotational grazing system or on pasture areas not suitable for crop production.
c. Chickens will be raised in mobile coops or free-range systems.
d. Cows and other animals can also be incorporated for meat production based on local population needs

3. **Fish Production:**

   a. The farm will incorporate small-scale aquaculture, producing fish such as tilapia or catfish in ponds or recirculating aquaculture systems.

   b. Fish waste will be used to fertilize crop fields or incorporated into compost.

4. **Egg Production:**

   a. The farm will maintain a flock of approximately 500 laying hens to produce eggs for the community.

   b. Hens will be raised in mobile coops or free-range systems.

5. **Crop Production:**

   a. The farm will grow crops such as rice, maize, tropical fruits (e.g., mangoes, papayas), vegetables (e.g., tomatoes, cucumbers, peppers), and herbs to supplement the livestock diet and provide food for the community.

   b. Sustainable practices such as intercropping, mulching, and crop rotation will be employed.

   c. Diverse cropping systems will be implemented to enhance soil health and biodiversity.

6. Honey Production:

a. The farm will maintain beehives for honey production, utilizing native flowering plants and crops for forage.
b. Honey production will contribute to pollination services and provide an additional income source for the farm.

7. Sugar Production:

a. The farm will allocate a portion of land for sugar cane cultivation.
b. Sugar cane will be processed to produce sugar for both on-farm consumption and potential sale to the local community.

8. Agroforestry and Perennial Crops:

a. The farm will incorporate agroforestry systems with fruit trees like mango, banana, and papaya, providing additional food sources and habitat for wildlife.
b. Perennial crops such as cassava, sweet potatoes, and herbs will be integrated into crop rotations.

Estimates for Farm Size in Acres:

a. Dairy Production: Approximately 50-100 acres.
b. Meat Production (Pigs and Chickens): Approximately 50-100 acres.
c. Fish Production: Approximately 5-10 acres.

d. Egg Production: Approximately 5 acres.
e. Crop Production (including vegetables and fruits): Approximately 200-300 acres.
f. Honey Production: Integrated within the existing farm area.
g. Sugar Production: Additional land allocation depending on scale.

Total: Adding up these estimates, the farm might require approximately 462-817 acres of land to support the various livestock and crop enterprises, including honey and sugar production.

This integrated farm setup aims to provide a diverse range of food products sustainably while promoting environmental stewardship and community resilience in Thailand.

Integrated farm for a small community of 10,000 people in **Tanzania**. Here's how it might look:

Integrated Farm Setup for a Community in Tanzania:

1. Dairy Production:

a. The farm will have a dairy herd of approximately 50 dairy cows, including indigenous breeds such as Tanzanian Shorthorn Zebu.
b. Cows will be grazed on pasture and supplemented with stored forages during dry periods.
c. Manure from dairy cows will be composted and used as fertilizer for crop fields.

2. Meat Production:

a. The farm will raise approximately 200 goats and 200 chickens for meat production.
b. Goats and chickens will be raised in rotational grazing systems or on pasture areas not suitable for crop production.
c. Grazing patterns will be managed to optimize forage utilization and soil health.
d. Cows and other animals can also be incorporated for meat production based on local population needs

3. **Fish Production:**

a. The farm will incorporate small-scale aquaculture, producing fish such as Nile tilapia in ponds or recirculating aquaculture systems.
b. Fish waste will be used to fertilize crop fields or incorporated into compost.

4. **Egg Production:**

a. The farm will maintain a flock of approximately 500 laying hens to produce eggs for the community.
b. Hens will be raised in mobile coops or free-range systems.

5. **Crop Production:**

a. The farm will grow crops such as maize, rice, sorghum, cassava, vegetables (e.g., tomatoes, onions, beans), and fruits (e.g., bananas, mangoes, pineapples) to supplement the livestock diet and provide food for the community.
b. Sustainable practices such as intercropping, mulching, and crop rotation will be employed.
c. Diverse cropping systems will be implemented to enhance soil health and biodiversity.

6. Honey Production:

a. The farm will maintain beehives for honey production, utilizing native vegetation and flowering crops for forage.
b. Honey production will contribute to pollination services and provide an additional income source for the farm.

7. Sugar Production:

a. The farm will allocate a portion of land for sugar cane cultivation.
b. Sugar cane will be processed to produce sugar for both on-farm consumption and potential sale to the local community.

8. Agroforestry and Perennial Crops:

a. The farm will incorporate agroforestry systems with indigenous trees such as acacia and fruit trees like mango and banana, providing additional food sources and habitat for wildlife.
b. Perennial crops such as cassava, sweet potatoes, and bananas will be integrated into crop rotations.

Estimates for Farm Size in Acres:

a. Dairy Production: Approximately 50-100 acres.
b. Meat Production (Goats and Chickens): Approximately 50-100 acres.

c. Fish Production: Approximately 5-10 acres.
d. Egg Production: Approximately 5 acres.
e. Crop Production (including vegetables and fruits): Approximately 200-300 acres.
f. Honey Production: Integrated within the existing farm area.
g. Sugar Production: Additional land allocation depending on scale.

Total: Adding up these estimates, the farm might require approximately 462-817 acres of land to support the various livestock and crop enterprises, including honey and sugar production.

This integrated farm setup aims to provide a diverse range of food products sustainably while promoting environmental stewardship and community resilience in Tanzania.

Integrated farm for a small community of 10,000 people in **South Africa**. Here's how it might look:

Integrated Farm Setup for a Community in South Africa:

1. **Dairy Production:**

   a. The farm will have a dairy herd of approximately 50 dairy cows, including breeds suitable for South African conditions such as Holsteins or Jerseys.
   b. Cows will be grazed on pasture and supplemented with stored forages during dry periods.
   c. Manure from dairy cows will be composted and used as fertilizer for crop fields.

2. **Meat Production:**

   a. The farm will raise approximately 200 beef cattle and 200 sheep for meat production.
   b. Cattle and sheep will be raised in rotational grazing systems, utilizing both natural pastures and improved pastures.
   c. Grazing patterns will be managed to optimize forage utilization and soil health.
   d. Cows and other animals can also be incorporated for meat production based on local population needs

3. **Fish Production:**

a. The farm will incorporate small-scale aquaculture, producing fish such as tilapia or catfish in ponds or recirculating aquaculture systems.
b. Fish waste will be used to fertilize crop fields or incorporated into compost.

4. **Egg Production:**

a. The farm will maintain a flock of approximately 500 laying hens to produce eggs for the community.
b. Hens will be raised in mobile coops or free-range systems.

5. **Crop Production:**

a. The farm will grow crops such as maize, wheat, citrus fruits, grapes, vegetables (e.g., tomatoes, onions, carrots, peppers), and fruits (e.g., citrus, mangoes, avocados) to supplement the livestock diet and provide food for the community.
b. Sustainable practices such as conservation tillage, cover cropping, and agroforestry will be employed.
c. Diverse cropping systems will be implemented to enhance soil health and biodiversity.

6. **Honey Production:**

  a. The farm will maintain beehives for honey production, utilizing native vegetation and flowering crops for forage.
  b. Honey production will contribute to pollination services and provide an additional income source for the farm.

7. **Sugar Production:**

  a. The farm will allocate a portion of land for sugar cane cultivation.
  b. Sugar cane will be processed to produce sugar for both on-farm consumption and potential sale to the local community.

8. **Agroforestry and Perennial Crops:**

  a. The farm will incorporate agroforestry systems with indigenous trees such as acacia and fruit trees like citrus and mango, providing additional food sources and habitat for wildlife.
  b. Perennial crops such as grapes, olives, and citrus will be integrated into crop rotations.

Estimates for Farm Size in Acres:

  a. Dairy Production: Approximately 50-100 acres.
  b. Meat Production (Cattle and Sheep): Approximately 200-400 acres.
  c. Fish Production: Approximately 5-10 acres.

d. Egg Production: Approximately 5 acres.
e. Crop Production (including vegetables and fruits): Approximately 200-300 acres.
f. Honey Production: Integrated within the existing farm area.
g. Sugar Production: Additional land allocation depending on scale.

Total: Adding up these estimates, the farm might require approximately 462-817 acres of land to support the various livestock and crop enterprises, including honey and sugar production.

This integrated farm setup aims to provide a diverse range of food products sustainably while promoting environmental stewardship and community resilience in South Africa.

To estimate the **number of people needed** to farm the integrated farms for communities of 10,000 people in Germany, Thailand, South Africa, and Tanzania, and the equipment required, we'll consider the various components of the farm and the tasks associated with each.

Estimated Number of People Needed:

1. **Germany:**

    * With a total farm size of approximately 225-397 acres (90.80-160.49 hectares), including dairy, meat, egg, fish, and crop production, as well as agroforestry, it could require a team of 20-30 skilled workers to manage the operations efficiently. This includes dairy workers, livestock handlers, crop farmers, aquaculturists, and general farm laborers.

2. **Thailand:**

    * For a farm size of approximately 100-200 acres (40.47-80.94 hectares), the labor requirement might be slightly higher due to the need for intensive management practices. A team of 30-40 workers could be necessary to handle dairy, meat, egg, fish, crop, and agroforestry production, including specialized skills in tropical agriculture and aquaculture.

3. **South Africa:**

- With a farm size of approximately 227-397 acres (91.86-160.49 hectares), similar to Germany, it would require a workforce of 20-30 skilled individuals to manage dairy, meat, egg, fish, crop, and agroforestry operations efficiently. However, additional labor might be needed for extensive grazing management, especially for cattle and sheep.

4. **Tanzania:**

- For a farm size of approximately 227-397 acres (91.86-160.49 hectares), it could require a larger workforce due to labor-intensive practices common in smallholder farming systems. A team of 40-50 workers might be necessary to manage dairy, meat, egg, fish, crop, and agroforestry production, including tasks such as hand harvesting and manual labor.

Equipment Needed:

1. **General Farm Equipment:**

- Tractors and implements for land preparation, planting, and harvesting.
- Irrigation equipment such as pumps, pipes, and sprinklers.
- Hand tools for manual labor and crop maintenance.

2. **Livestock Equipment:**

- Milking machines and cooling tanks for dairy production.
- Feed mixers and dispensers for livestock feeding.
- Mobile coops and housing structures for chickens and pigs.
- Pond liners and aeration systems for aquaculture.

3. **Crop Equipment:**

- Planters and seeders for crop planting.
- Sprayers for pest and weed control.
- Harvesters for crops such as maize, wheat, and fruits.
- Storage facilities for crop storage and processing.

4. **Agroforestry Equipment:**

- Pruning tools for tree maintenance.
- Harvesting equipment for fruits and nuts.
- Mulchers and chippers for organic matter management.

Overall, the specific equipment requirements would vary based on farm size, production methods, and technological advancements available in each region. Additionally, training and capacity building programs may be necessary to ensure the efficient and sustainable operation of the integrated farms.

Germany:

- Population: Approximately 83 million (as of 2022).
- Number of farms needed: 83 million/ 10000= 8,300 farms.
- Assuming each farm requires a team of 20-30 skilled workers, let's use the midpoint of 25 workers per farm.
- Total number of workers: 8,300 farms × 25 workers/farm = 207,500 workers.

Thailand:

- Population: Approximately 69 million (as of 2022).
- Number of farms needed: 69 million/10000 = 6,900 farms.
- Assuming each farm requires a team of 30-40 workers, let's use the midpoint of 35 workers per farm.
- Total number of workers: 6,900 farms × 35 workers/farm = 241,500 workers.

South Africa:

- Population: Approximately 60 million (as of 2022).
- Number of farms needed: 60 million/10000 = 6,000 farms.

- Assuming each farm requires a team of 20-30 skilled workers, let's use the midpoint of 25 workers per farm.
- Total number of workers: 6,000 farms × 25 workers/farm = 150,000 workers.

Tanzania:

- Population: Approximately 61 million (as of 2022).
- Number of farms needed: 61 million/10000 = 6,100 farms.
- Assuming each farm requires a team of 40-50 workers, let's use the midpoint of 45 workers per farm.
- Total number of workers: 6,100 farms × 45 workers/farm = 274,500 workers.

These estimates provide an approximate idea of the workforce required to manage the integrated farms for each country. Actual workforce requirements may vary based on factors such as farm size, production methods, and labor efficiency.

The calculations above offer a preliminary glimpse into the labor force needed to cultivate integrated farms in Germany, Thailand, South Africa, and Tanzania under the PEOPLEIZE Agriculture Future framework. By considering each country's population size and the estimated number of farms required to sustainably feed its inhabitants, we can approximate the workforce necessary to manage these agricultural operations.

In Germany, with a population of approximately 83 million, an estimated 8,300 farms would be needed to support local food production. Assuming each farm requires a team of 20-30 skilled workers, the total workforce required amounts to 207,500 individuals. These workers would be responsible for implementing sustainable farming practices, managing livestock, cultivating crops, and ensuring the smooth operation of each integrated farm. Additionally, each farmer would receive an equal salary of €50,000, resulting in a total annual cost of €10,375,000,000 for the government.

Similarly, in Thailand, with a population of roughly 69 million, an estimated 6,900 farms would be necessary to meet local food demands. With each farm employing a team of 30-40 workers, the total workforce required is projected to be around 241,500 individuals. These workers would play a pivotal role in advancing agricultural sustainability, enhancing food security, and fostering community resilience. Each farmer would receive an equal salary of 50,000 Thai baht, resulting in a total annual cost of 12,075,000,000 Thai baht for the government.

In South Africa, with a population of approximately 60 million, an estimated 6,000 farms would be required to support local food production. Assuming each farm requires a team of 20-30 skilled workers, the total workforce needed is estimated at 150,000 individuals. These workers would contribute to revitalizing rural economies, promoting sustainable land management practices, and ensuring equitable access to nutritious food for all. Each farmer would receive an equal salary of 50,000 South African rand, resulting in a total annual cost of 7,500,000,000 South African rand for the government.

In Tanzania, with a population of around 61 million, an estimated 6,100 farms would be needed to sustainably feed its inhabitants. With each farm employing a team of 40-50 workers, the total workforce required is projected to be approximately 274,500 individuals. These workers would be instrumental in implementing agroecological principles, conserving natural resources, and promoting inclusive agricultural development. Each farmer would receive an equal salary of 50,000 Tanzanian shillings, resulting in a total annual cost of 13,725,000,000 Tanzanian shillings for the government.

While these estimates provide a foundational understanding of the workforce needed for integrated farming in each country, it's essential to recognize that actual labor requirements may vary based on numerous factors. Factors such as farm size, production methods, technological advancements, and labor efficiency will influence the precise number of workers needed to manage these agricultural operations effectively.

Nonetheless, these projections underscore the significant role that a skilled and dedicated workforce will play in realizing the vision of sustainable, community-centered agriculture in each country.

In addition to estimating the annual cost of providing equal salaries to farmers in Germany, Thailand, South Africa, and Tanzania, it's important to contextualize these costs in comparison to the military budgets of each respective country. Furthermore, we can highlight the numerous benefits that communities derive from the efforts of farmers within the PEOPLEIZE Agriculture Future framework.

In Germany, where the government would incur an annual cost of €10,375,000,000 to provide equal salaries to farmers, it's enlightening to compare this expense to the country's military budget. Germany allocated approximately €52 billion to its military in 2022, highlighting a significant contrast in resource allocation between defense spending and agricultural development. By redirecting a portion of military funds towards supporting farmers, the government can foster greater food security, environmental sustainability, and community resilience.

Similarly, in Thailand, where the government would spend approximately 12,075,000,000 Thai baht annually on equal farmer salaries, it's noteworthy that the country allocated around 227 billion Thai baht to its military in 2022. This stark difference underscores the potential for reallocating resources towards agricultural initiatives that benefit local communities and promote inclusive economic growth. By prioritizing investment in sustainable agriculture, Thailand can enhance food sovereignty, mitigate rural poverty, and strengthen social cohesion.

In South Africa, where the government would allocate roughly 7,500,000,000 South African rand per year for equal farmer salaries, it's pertinent to compare this expenditure to the country's military budget. South Africa earmarked approximately 48 billion South African rand for defense purposes in 2022, indicating a significant opportunity to repurpose funds towards supporting small-scale farmers and rural development. By investing in agriculture, South Africa can address food insecurity, create employment opportunities, and foster environmental stewardship.

In Tanzania, where the government would spend around 13,725,000,000 Tanzanian shillings annually on equal farmer salaries, it's essential to consider this cost alongside the country's military budget. Tanzania allocated approximately 1.8 trillion Tanzanian shillings to its military in 2022, highlighting a substantial disparity in resource allocation between defense spending and agricultural development. By reallocating a portion of military funds towards supporting farmers, Tanzania can enhance food production, alleviate poverty, and promote sustainable livelihoods.

Beyond the financial considerations, communities benefit immensely from the efforts of farmers within the PEOPLEIZE Decolonization Agriculture framework. By transitioning to integrated farming practices, communities become more self-sufficient, reducing reliance on external food sources and enhancing food security. Moreover, the implementation of renewable energy systems, waste recycling initiatives, and water treatment facilities on integrated farms contributes to environmental sustainability and resource conservation. Additionally, hyper-local farming fosters stronger community bonds, as residents collaborate to meet their collective food needs, share resources, and support local economies. Overall, investing in agriculture not only improves livelihoods and strengthens communities but also lays the foundation for a more resilient and equitable society.

In the forthcoming volumes of our series, we will delve deeper into the intricacies of government and legal decolonization and their intersection with each aspect of the PEOPLEIZE Decolonization Agriculture framework. We aim to elucidate how empowering individuals to govern themselves, not as mere servants but as active participants in a global government, is paramount to achieving true equity and justice.

Through a comprehensive exploration of governance structures, legal frameworks, and participatory decision-making processes, we seek to empower communities to reclaim their agency and shape their destinies in alignment with the principles of decolonization.

Moreover, as we continue our journey towards decolonization, we will explore innovative approaches to address historical injustices, dismantle oppressive systems, and foster genuine collaboration and solidarity among diverse communities worldwide. By embracing the ethos of WOBUNTU "I Am, Because We Are," we recognize the interconnectedness of humanity and the imperative of collective action in advancing the common good. Through dialogue, education, and advocacy, we aspire to cultivate a global consciousness rooted in collaboration, equity, and mutual respect.

As we embark on this transformative journey, we invite readers to join us in envisioning and co-creating a world where every individual is valued, empowered, and afforded equal opportunities to thrive. Together, we can harness the power of PEOPLEIZE to build a more just, inclusive, and sustainable future for generations to come.

MY HEARTFELT GRATITUDE

In the quiet moments of reflection as I write these words for "PEOPLEIZE," my heart swells with gratitude. This book, an exploration of collaboration, peaceful community, sustainability, and the pursuit of shared prosperity, has been a journey unlike any other. To each reader who has embarked on this odyssey with me, I offer my sincerest thanks.

To those who have dared to challenge the norms, to dream boldly, and to imagine a world where unity reigns supreme, your unwavering commitment to this vision has been the driving force behind "PEOPLEIZE." I am deeply grateful for your courage and your willingness to push the boundaries of what is possible.

Creating a work of this magnitude is never a solitary effort. I am immensely thankful to the countless individuals who have contributed, in ways both large and small, to the realization of "PEOPLEIZE." Your insights, your support, and your shared passion have been instrumental in bringing this vision to life.

To the visionaries who believe in the transformative power of collaboration, to those who champion for equality, justice and understanding, and to every advocate for a more equitable world, this book is a testament to our shared ideals. May the ideas contained within its pages inspire dialogue, action, and positive change in the world.

To all who hold fast to the belief in a future where peace, equality, harmony and prosperity are shared by all, I extend my deepest gratitude. "PEOPLEIZE" is more than just a book; it is a beacon of hope for a brighter tomorrow. Thank you for joining me on this incredible journey.

With heartfelt appreciation and warm wishes,
xoxo Einar